science fair winners

BUG SCIENCE

20 projects and experiments about
arthropods: insects, arachnids, algae, worms,
and other small creatures

by Karen Romano Young

Illustrations by David Goldin

NATIONAL GEOGRAPHIC

WASHINGTON, D.C.

credits

All illustraton by David Goldin

PUBLISHED BY THE NATIONAL GEOGRAPHIC SOCIETY

John M. Fahey, Jr., *President and Chief Executive Officer*
Gilbert M. Grosvenor, *Chairman of the Board*
Tim T. Kelly, President, *Global Media Group*
John Q. Griffin, *Executive Vice President; President, Publishing*
Nina D. Hoffman, *Executive Vice President; President, Book Publishing Group*
Melina Gerosa Bellows, *Executive Vice President, Children's Publishing*

PREPARED BY THE BOOK DIVISION

Nancy Laties Feresten, *Vice President, Editor in Chief, Children's Books*
Jonathan Halling, *Director of Design, Children's Publishing*
Jennifer Emmett, *Executive Editor, Children's Books*
Carl Mehler, *Director of Maps*
R. Gary Colbert, *Production Director*
Jennifer A. Thornton, *Managing Editor*

STAFF FOR THIS BOOK

Amy Shields, Priyanka Lamichhane, *Editors*
Bea Jackson, Director of Design and Illustration-
James Hiscott, Jr., *Art Director / Designer*
Grace Hill, *Associate Managing Editor*
Lewis R. Bassford, *Production Manager*
Susan Borke, *Legal and Business Affairs*

MANUFACTURING AND QUALITY MANAGEMENT

Christopher A. Liedel, *Chief Financial Officer*
Phillip L. Schlosser, *Vice President*
Chris Brown, *Technical Director*
Nicole Elliott, *Manager*
Rachel Faulise, *Manager*

The National Geographic Society is one of the world's largest nonprofit scientific and educational organizations. Founded in 1888 to "increase and diffuse geographic knowledge," the Society works to inspire people to care about the planet. It reaches more than 325 million people worldwide each month through its official journal, *National Geographic*, and other magazines; National Geographic Channel; television documentaries; music; radio; films; books; DVDs; maps; exhibitions; school publishing programs; interactive media; and merchandise. National Geographic has funded more than 9,000 scientific research, conservation and exploration projects and supports an education program combating geographic illiteracy. For more information, visit nationalgeographic.com.

For more information, please call 1-800-NGS LINE (647-5463) or write to the following address:
National Geographic Society
1145 17th Street N.W.
Washington, D.C. 20036-4688 U.S.A.

Visit us online at www.nationalgeographic.com/books
For librarians and teachers: www.ngchildrensbooks.org
More for kids from National Geographic:
kids.nationalgeographic.com
For information about special discounts for bulk purchases, please contact National Geographic Books Special Sales:
ngspecsales@ngs.org
For rights or permissions inquiries, please contact National Geographic Books Subsidiary Rights: ngbookrights@ngs.org

Library of Congress Cataloging-in-Publication Data
Young, Karen Romano.
  Science fair winners -- bug science : 20 projects and experiments about arthropods: insects, arachnids, algae, worms, and other small creatures / by Karen Romano Young. -- 1st ed.
    p. cm. -- (Science fair winners)
  Includes bibliographical references and index.
  ISBN 978-1-4263-0519-1 (pbk. : alk. paper) -- ISBN 978-1-4263-0520-7 (library binding : alk. paper)
  1. Arthropoda--Juvenile literature. 2. Science projects--Juvenile literature. I. Title.
  QL434.15.Y68 2009
  595.7078--dc22
                                    2009012734

09/WOR/1

THE WORKSHOPS

WELCOME TO BUG SCIENCE

the introduction

BUG SCIENCE is dedicated to helping you design a science project that will wow your teachers, the crowd at your science fair, and anyone else who hears about it.

The projects in *Bug Science* let you study many aspects of the life of an arthropod (an animal with six or more jointed legs), while showing you all kinds of science involving bugs.

You'll learn to:

- ask a question and turn it into a study;
- make observations, make comparisons, and draw conclusions (the building blocks of the scientific method), while also leading you to. . .
- do your own research based on the work of scientists who are doing great projects in the fields of entomology (the study of insects), arachnology (the study of spiders), biology, chemistry, physics, psychology, sociology, economics, agriculture, and more.

Don't be surprised if you fall in love with bugs and all the different kinds of science they inspire.

which workshop?

Some of the workshops are experiments, because lots of science fairs require you to do an experiment. Some of them are observations and surveys, because real scientists don't just do experiments. Their work also falls into the two categories of observation and surveying. Here's a way to think about the differences:

You **experiment** when you change something in a situation and observe and survey the outcome.

You **observe** when you find a bug, notice the place where you found it, and watch it to see what it does.

You **survey** when you look to see what other bugs there are, count them, and notice how many are doing similar things. In other words, you repeat your observation to see if it reveals a pattern.

Some of the workshops seem really science-y. Some of them don't. This might be because you define science in terms of nature: biology (the study of life), chemistry (the

Arthropods emerge from eggs as pupae, mature into larvae, and then become adults through metamorphosis. Although this is the basic life cycle, there are many variations. For example, some hatchlings look like miniature adults; others show no resemblance to the adults they'll become.

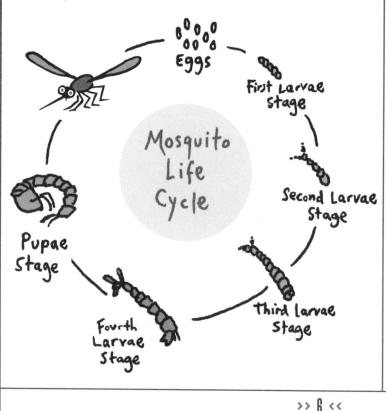

Mosquito Life Cycle

Eggs

First Larvae Stage

Second Larvae Stage

Third Larvae Stage

Fourth Larvae Stage

Pupae Stage

elements), or physics (time, space, motion, and so on). But this book includes workshops that look at bugs through social sciences, too. These include psychology (what's in someone's head), sociology (how a group and members of a group behave), anthropology (the study of humans), and economics (the science of money and business).

Some of the workshops seem hard, and others seem easy. This might depend on what you find easy to do and what makes you nervous. It's all good science, though. If you're not sure whether a workshop will satisfy science fair requirements, ask before you get started.

What if. . .? I wonder. . .? How can I find out. . .?

These three question starters are the beginnings of all science. They lead to observing, experimenting, reaching a conclusion, and finding another question, which leads you to more science and more watching, testing, and understanding, which leads to another question. . . . Well, you get the idea.

finding bugs

Where do I get bugs to study?
At pet shops and insect suppliers. Check the Internet to find insects you can buy and have shipped to you. Take note of the advice from these experts about the food and equipment the insects require. You can also look around the house, park, school, trash, woods, and fields.

What bugs live around me?
As you look at populations (different species) and representation (how many of each species) you'll gain understanding of the biodiversity (different kinds of bugs) in your area at different times of year. Insects show up seasonally. For example, in Maryland grasshoppers show up in August and September, luna moths in early May and again in late August, and certain flies in April or May. What's the insect calendar where you live?

How do I catch bugs?
- Set out a paper plate with molasses or honey on it. Watch to see what comes.
- Hang a sheet on a clothesline. Let the bottom of the sheet hang into a jar. Bugs that fly into the sheet will slide down into the jar.
- Go hunting with a butterfly net.
- Use a sweep net in tall grass or under trees. (Sweep nets are available from wildlife suppliers.)
- Shake low-hanging bushes or trees. Let the bugs fall into a net, sheet, or upside-down umbrella.
- Leave an outside light on all night. In the morning, examine the dead bugs.

How do I stay safe around bugs?

Know your allergies. Some people are deathly allergic to bees. If you're not sure, avoid bees. Wear insect repellent. Have over-the-counter medications on hand to soothe your skin if you are bitten.

keeping bugs

How do I keep my bugs (alive)?

If you buy bugs, follow the advice of the pet store or insect supplier.

If you find your bugs outside, keep them in a jar, aquarium, or other container where they can be kept separate from people. Catch and release, or keep them to observe.

Do research to identify your bugs and figure out what kind of food they need to eat. If it's a leaf eater, such as a caterpillar, bring along some leaves from the plant or tree you found it on. Flies may be fed dried milk, sugar, or dog food (See Workshop 1: Raise Your Own); spiders may be fed flies.

Assume nothing about the nervous system of another creature. Scientists aren't sure how much pain bugs feel. Be kind. Consider whether you really can figure out the effects of things like heavy metal music, extreme temperatures, or dangerous substances on a living thing. Unless you're breaking new ground in science, don't conduct such experiments just to get a grade.

> **Certain bugs are protected, such as the praying mantis, which is the state insect of Connecticut. Don't kill 'em.**

How do I keep my bugs (dead)?

Use a small box with a lid, a clear jar, or a small plastic craft box. Craft boxes, made for storing beads and other tiny items, work well for holding and displaying bugs, and they may even have a lid that magnifies the contents. Museum shops and science suppliers also have small containers with magnifying lids. Some collectors glue or pin dead bugs to wood or cardboard.

How do I keep the environment safe?

Never introduce strange bugs to your environment. Most habitats have a problem with invasive species—organisms that have been introduced to the area but that don't belong there. Problems include invasive species eating food that usually is eaten by something else, invasive species having no natural predators, and invasive species eating the eggs of native species.

So if you order or buy bugs, don't just let them go when your experiment is over. Ask the store or supplier what to do with bugs you use. It is better for the environment as a whole to kill a bug than to put it in an area where it has no predators or where it might prey on food that other creatures depend on.

identifying bugs

Use a guidebook or website to identify your bug. See *The Resources* (p. 78).

If you can't find your exact bug, choose one characteristic and try to find other bugs that share this characteristic. For example, look at wings. Does your insect have one pair of wings or two? If it has one, then its order is Diptera (true flies). If it has two pairs of wings, you'll need to ask more questions to narrow down its order. Look at the other orders of insects, focusing on the wings. Which ones have wings like your bug's?

As you narrow the choices, note where the guide or website leads you and look at other characteristics. Note: Using several different websites and guidebooks lets you cross-check your information.

id iq: resources

- Insect zoos: in person or online. See *The Resources* (p. 78).
- Pet stores: They sell a variety of bugs as food for the pets they sell. They can sometimes help you identify your own bugs. Call before you bring in a bug!
- University extensions, 4-H extensions, and other agricultural extensions. If you have one of these nearby and can take or send your live or dead bug there, you can get expert bug identification, as well as information about your bug's range (where it normally lives), what it eats, what preys on it, what diseases it might carry, and so on.
- Pest control services can also provide expertise. They get rid of pesky bugs, and they're good at identifying them, too.
- Websites: Use an Internet search tool like Google. Type in the kind of insect you think it might be (use the family, such as a click beetle). Images on the Web might give you a hint of how to identify your bug. See *The Resources* (p. 78) for additional sites.

if all else fails

What if you find something that you think is a new species? If you're not sure what you've got, or if you think you've found a new species, take a digital photo of your bug and send the JPEG or TIFF file to Gary Hevel at the Smithsonian: GHevel@si.edu.

RAISE YOUR OWN

(Raise flies)

TIME NEEDED ›
19–70 days

SCIENCE › entomology

SCIENCE CONCEPTS ›
life cycle, food chain, development, behavior, nutrition

ADULT INVOLVEMENT ›
permission to raise flies and a place away from living areas in which to do it

the basics

THE AVERAGE HOUSEFLY lives 19 to 70 days. During most of this time, the housefly is in its adult phase, mating, finding food, and using the food it finds to create a medium for laying its eggs.

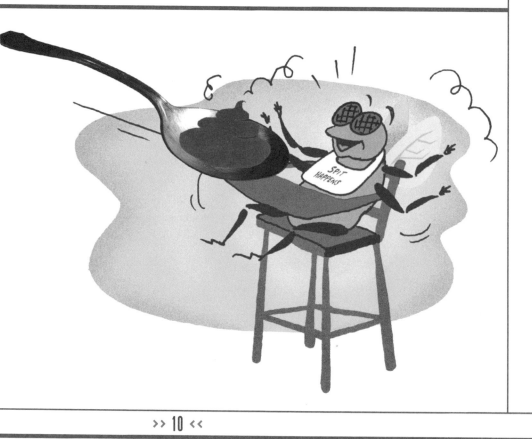

the QUESTION >>

Can you raise houseflies through a complete life cycle?

the PLAN >>

You can start with adult flies and care for them as they mate and lay eggs, or begin with larvae (maggots) and care for them until they develop into adult flies. The point is to find out whether you can witness and record a life cycle, and to notice the conditions under which it happens.

the buzz

Two Texas Cooperative Extension scientists, Dr. Greta Schuster and Dr. Jeff Tomberlin, raised three generations of flies and studied their resistance to pesticides. They found that flies are more resistant to pesticides when more is used. Their research has led them to advise people to use pesticides only when there's a bug problem, not "just in case."

the lingo

larva—the second stage of development for an insect; larvae hatch from eggs
pupa—the third stage of development for an insect; pupae "rest" before emerging into full adult form
adult—the last stage of an insect's life; the end of its metamorphosis
metamorphosis—an insect's development from egg to adult insect
medium—a substance allowing for life

⌄ Housefly life cycle

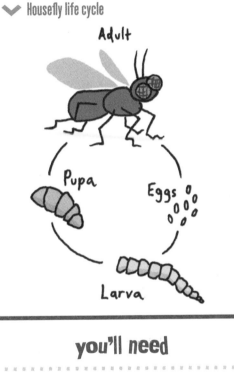

you'll need

houseflies or maggots—see Catch a Fly (p. 12) for advice on finding them
a fly trap jar—any jar, its opening covered with nylon stocking fabric or fine mesh screening
3 small jar lids—baby food jar lids are ideal

a fly house—a lidded container big enough to hold lids for food, egg-laying medium, and water

fly food—Combine one teaspoon each of dried milk and sugar. Add water to make a stiff paste. Place a dab in a jar lid. You can also use raw hamburger.

fly water—wet cotton ball or cosmetic pad placed on a jar lid

egg-laying medium—Soak one tablespoon of dry dog food in warm water for five minutes. Then drain the water. Mix the damp dog food with a quarter of a bag of yeast (or a piece of a cake). Keep the medium moist by adding a little water. Flies will lay their eggs there; fly larvae (maggots) that hatch can eat it.

what to do

1 **CATCH A FLY.** *Human flytraps:* Place some fly food in a small jar. When a fly comes, capture it with a piece of screen or the lid. *Superhuman flytraps:* You can catch flies in your bare hand. Do you have to be quick? Yes. Do you have to keep a space inside your fist? You do. Can you do it with practice? Only you can determine this.

NOTE: *If you are raising flies in order to feed them to spiders or reptiles, you can trap a few at a time from your fly house. Fold back the fly house cover and place a jar in the open-*

ing. Flies will climb up into the jar. After they do, slip a card or an old CD across the opening of the jar, remove the jar, and replace the fly house cover.

2 **SET UP YOUR FLY HOUSE WITH FOOD, WATER, AND EGG-LAYING MEDIUM.** Be sure to record how many flies are in your fly house when your experiment starts.

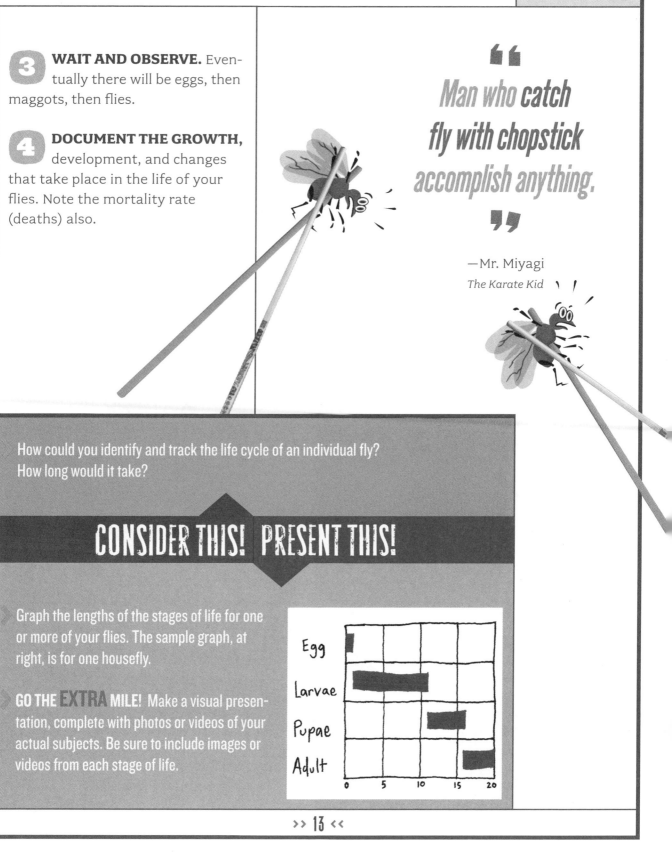

3 **WAIT AND OBSERVE.** Eventually there will be eggs, then maggots, then flies.

4 **DOCUMENT THE GROWTH,** development, and changes that take place in the life of your flies. Note the mortality rate (deaths) also.

> " Man who **catch fly with chopstick** accomplish anything. "

—Mr. Miyagi
The Karate Kid

How could you identify and track the life cycle of an individual fly? How long would it take?

CONSIDER THIS! PRESENT THIS!

> Graph the lengths of the stages of life for one or more of your flies. The sample graph, at right, is for one housefly.

> **GO THE EXTRA MILE!** Make a visual presentation, complete with photos or videos of your actual subjects. Be sure to include images or videos from each stage of life.

SWIMMING IN IT

(Observe microscopic bugs)

TIME NEEDED ›
one day

SCIENCE ›
microbiology

SCIENCE CONCEPTS ›
population assessment,
laboratory procedures

ADULT INVOLVEMENT ›
permission to borrow
a microscope and video
camera temporarily (see
Video It, p. 78), and a ride
to a local water source,
if needed

the basics

THAT GREEN SCUM on the surface of still water is phytoplankton called cyanobacteria—tiny, one-celled blue-green algae that turn sunlight into oxygen. They created our atmosphere through this process, and they help maintain the levels of oxygen needed in the air and in water. Cyanobacteria support all the life on Earth.

From algae to barely visible water bears and the nymphs of water bugs, mayflies, and dragonflies, the water may be teeming with life.

the QUESTION >>

What microscopic organisms live in a sample of pond or sea water?

the PLAN >>

Use a magnifying lens or microscope to survey the population of (what's living in) a sample of fresh or salt water, to observe these individuals, and to count their representation (how many individuals of each kind there are).

the buzz

Satellites are used to measure the levels of algae in oceans and other bodies of water. Levels of algae are important indicators of where fish will be—since big fish feed on little fish, which feed on zooplankton, which feed on algae. Big changes over time in algae levels are indicators of climate changes.

the lingo

phytoplankton—algae that absorb light to make food (photosynthesis)

zooplankton—algae that feed on smaller algae such as phytoplankton or other zooplankton

you'll need

magnifying lens, dissecting microscope; flexi-cam (a camera that shows objects at magnification on your television screen) **or video camera** (you don't need both!)
small jars—to collect water samples
masking tape—to label on jars where water samples come from
petri dish or other shallow glass or clear plastic dish—to hold your samples

what to do

1 **CHOOSE A BODY OF WATER** to sample, observe, and assess (count).
NOTE: *View and examine your sample as soon as possible. Things might die or be eaten by other individuals in the water.*

2 **TAKE CAREFUL NOTE OF THE LOCATION AND CONDITIONS** where you took your sample. Map it. Then jot down time, the air and water temperature, and other observable or measurable characteristics.

3 **OBSERVE YOUR SAMPLE(S) WITH YOUR NAKED EYE.** Make note of anything you can find alive. Try to isolate it by placing it in a separate dish. (This big creature might eat the smaller ones.) Observe your sample with the magnifying lens, the flexi-cam, and the dissecting microscope.

4 **DRAW EACH KIND OF ORGANISM YOU OBSERVE,** and count to find the population of each kind in your sample.

WORKSHOP RESOURCE >>
The Smallest Page on the Web
www.microscopy-uk.org.uk/index.html?http://www.microscopy-uk.org.uk/pond

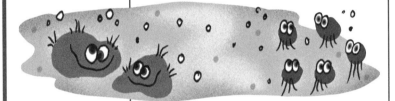

Sample and compare water from different parts of one water source, different water sources, and at different times of day and night.

CONSIDER THIS! PRESENT THIS!

Make a table showing the sorts of creatures you identified (the population) and how many there were (the representation). Include your drawings, and be sure to display your videos.

GO THE EXTRA MILE! Take a sample from still water near a source of pollutants (road or fertilizer run-off). Compare it with water you think is clean.

ANTS COME MARCHING

(Try to make an ant get lost)

the basics

ANTS, **LIKE SPIDERS,** rodents, and humans, keep track of where they are, where they're going, and how to get there. They remember the turns they take, as well as the uphills and downhills, as they cross an area.

TIME NEEDED ›
one day

SCIENCE ›
entomology, geography

SCIENCE CONCEPTS›
path integration, navigation, behavior

ADULT INVOLVEMENT ›
Certain ants (such as fire ants and red ants) may sting. That doesn't mean you shouldn't study them, only that common sense and supervision are needed.

the buzz

Scientists at Humboldt University in Berlin, Germany, experimented to see what would happen if ants had to travel through high hills and valleys (verticals) as well as going east, west, north, and south (horizontals). They tried adding hills and other obstructions to the ants' habitats to see if they would still be able to "home" (find their destination), and the ants did fine at finding their way.

the lingo

orient—to figure out which direction you are facing

navigate—to figure out a route and follow it

you'll need

ant bait—a jar lid with sugar water, maple syrup, honey, or jam

an obstruction—an object to block the path of the ants. Try a book, pieces of wood, or a stack of building blocks. Your purpose is to see if ants can find their way after meeting your obstruction, not to keep them from going over it.

what to do

1 **FIND ANTS.** In cool or warm weather, you should be able to find ants in the wild and do the experiment where they are. You don't need to capture them. Just follow them and figure out where they're going. Determine their starting point (probably the anthill) and their destination (probably a food source). If you can't find ants, or if it's winter, use ants from an ant farm.

2 **SET THE BAIT.** Note what the ants do. Do they approach the bait, investigate it, and go away to find the other ants and let them know? This is the pattern that ants usually follow. Try to observe it. Follow the ants that go away, and find out what they do.

3 **WATCH YOUR ANTS CLOSELY.** Take pictures or video to add to your data.

- Find the anthill. You will want to map this area, so take careful measurements.
- You might consider drawing a

the QUESTION >> Will an ant diverted or moved off course find its way to its goal?

the PLAN >> Get ants off track and observe their response, measuring the routes they take to locate food or their anthill.

chalk line behind an ant to trace its path back and forth from the anthill to the bait.

4 **WHILE YOU'RE OBSERVING...** Once your ants have oriented themselves and have created a path to the bait, see if you can time one ant in its unobstructed path from anthill to bait.

5 **CLOCK THEIR MOVEMENTS.** You have drawn ants to your bait, and these ants have taken the information about your bait's location back to their anthill and left a scent trail for their colony to follow. Now put up your obstruction. Observe what the ants do. Again, try to trace the path of one ant, and time it to see how long it takes for it to go from the anthill to the food source. Time how long it takes for the ant to cross the obstruction.

6 **ANALYZE ANTS.** Carefully note what the ants do when they reach the ground again after crossing the obstruction. Do they seem confused? Do they go the wrong way? How long does it take them to figure out the right way? Do your ants eventually learn the new path over the obstruction?

7 **NOW, REMOVE THE OBSTRUCTION.** Carefully note what happens!

WORKSHOP RESOURCE >>
Richard Feynman's book *Surely You're Joking, Mr. Feynman* has a wonderful chapter about the Nobel Prize-winning physicist's experiments with ants.

Some ants may go around your obstruction to stay on flat ground. Try to set up the obstruction differently so that they can't or won't do this. Try digging a trench. Line it with colored construction paper and cover it with glass from an old picture frame. Will the ants follow the path or try to go around?

CONSIDER THIS! PRESENT THIS!

Make a model of your ants' area, complete with a miniature of your obstruction.

GO THE EXTRA MILE! Map the route that the ants took between the anthill and the food source. Consider using contour markings to show your obstruction's height. (Contour markings show the elevation of an area; each contour marking stands for a certain number of feet or inches.)

HONEY, HELP ME WITH THIS HAY FEVER!

(Try to reduce hay fever by eating local honey)

TIME NEEDED >
several weeks, months, or even a year!

SCIENCE >
entomology, medicine, nutrition

SCIENCE CONCEPTS >
pollen, allergies

ADULT INVOLVEMENT >
permission to try alternative hay fever treatments

>> Check with your teacher before involving human subjects in your science fair workshops.

the basics

BEES GO FROM FLOWER TO FLOWER sipping nectar—a sugary, watery substance produced by flowers that also contains some pollen. To produce one pound of honey, bees take nectar from two million flowers. Honey is actually bee vomit. It's what honeybees regurgitate after eating pollen. They produce it to feed their young and also to eat during the winter.

the buzz

If you eat honey, you take pollen into your body. This doesn't cause an allergic reaction because you're eating it, not breathing it in, but it gets into your body all the same. Some scientists think eating local pollen in honey may immunize your body against having an allergic reaction to local pollen you breathe in.

NOTE: *Pollen levels might affect people differently, depending on their allergies and their use of local honey.*

the lingo

pollen—a powderlike material produced by flowers; it's required in fertilizing plants

immunize—to stop from responding; an immunization stops your body from responding to an invading germ so you don't get sick

you'll need

local honey—Check a local farm stand or orchard. Read the label on the jar to determine whether the honey is actually made nearby. You might also look in the phone book yellow pages under "apiary" or "beekeeping." Grocery stores or health food stores may also sell local honey. Find honey from bees nearest to your house.

the QUESTION >> Can eating local honey reduce hay fever?

the PLAN >> Conduct an experiment on your own body to see if eating honey from local bees affects your pollen allergy.

what to do

1 **GET A BASELINE.** Ideally you'd work on this project for at least two growing seasons, taking one season to record your experiences with allergic reactions before trying the preventive treatment of eating local honey, then

> **"**
> *I don't know if it's **true or not** but lots of people swear **that my honey** makes hay fever better.*
> **"**
>
> —Tim Haarmaan
> *Los Alamos National Laboratory, scientist and beekeeper*

ACHOooo

beginning to eat local honey and recording allergic reactions afterward. ***NOTE:*** *Much of scientific research does take this long!*

Write a statement describing your feelings on a typical day when your allergic reactions were high. How did you feel? How well could you breathe? What medications did you take, if any?

2 **EAT LOCAL HONEY REGULARLY.** Designate a certain amount of honey to eat per week. Recommended amount: two teaspoons of honey a day for a month before the regular pollen season in your area begins. If you have enough time, try eating honey this way for two or three months before pollen season.

3 **TAKE NOTE OF YOUR REACTIONS TO THE ONSET OF POLLEN SEASON.** Compare them to reactions from previous years.

WORKSHOP RESOURCE >>
To get the pollen count in your location:
www.pollen.com

Get a group of hay fever sufferers and measure their responses. Do you have a cousin who lives in another part of the country? See if he or she would like to do this long-term science experiment with you!

CONSIDER THIS! PRESENT THIS!

Graph your responses alongside data showing the pollen count.

GO THE EXTRA MILE! Create an advertisement for local honey suppliers, using your experiment results as material.

WATCHING SPIDERS

(Observe a spider in captivity)

the basics

THERE ARE MORE THAN 34,000 species of spiders, including ones that live in Antarctica and others that thrive in the craters of active volcanoes on the big island of Hawaii. There are spiders in every ecological environment in the world. Some are miniscule (2 to 10 millimeters long), and others are mammoth (up to 90 mm long). And they're all carnivores!

TIME NEEDED ›
a week or more

SCIENCE ›
arachnology, zoology

SCIENCE CONCEPTS ›
observation, habitats

ADULT INVOLVEMENT ›
Discuss your plans to catch and keep spiders. Get help identifying the spiders you adopt. Most areas have a few spiders whose bites are dangerous to people.

the buzz

New York City high school student Martin Romane counted more than 120 spiders per square yard of a grassy city lot. He observed the spiders he caught and created habitats for them. His first experiment with spiders involved tearing one strand of one web to see if the spider would notice. (What do you think happened?)

the lingo

habitat—an environment that supplies everything an organism needs

you'll need

a jar—with a wide mouth and a lid with holes poked in it

a butterfly net—for certain kinds of spiders (especially wolf spiders, which jump)

a stiff, thin piece of card or an old CD

a spider house—preferably an aquarium with a fine mesh screen lid (see *Keeping Bugs*, p. 8)

a notebook—for observations

a large funnel

the QUESTION >>

How does a spider behave in captivity? What can I discover about a spider by observing it daily over a period of time?

the PLAN >>

By meeting a spider's needs for space, temperature, food, and water, you can observe its habits and long-term changes.

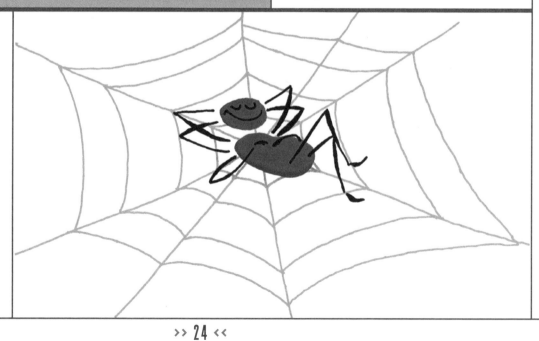

what to do

1 **FIND A SPIDER.** Spiders can be located on bushes, in drains, alongside ponds and pools, and under leaves. Inside the house, look in windowsills, corners, and the undersides of chairs. For more tips, see *Finding Bugs* (p. 7), or try these methods:

- Put a shovelful of old leaves into a funnel, and place the funnel in a jar. Shine a desk lamp on top, and any spiders in the leaves will crawl down into the funnel and drop into the jar.
- Bury an empty soup can up to its rim to make a pit trap. Camouflage it with leaves or branches.
- Find a web, and you will usually find a spider nearby. Notice the size of the web. A spider with a bigger web needs a bigger habitat.

2 **INTRODUCE THE SPIDER TO THE SPIDER HOUSE.**

To make the inside of your aquarium resemble the place where you found the spider, add branches, sand, dirt, rocks, or leaves. Keep the spider house out of the sun. Spiders appreciate shade and indirect light. Place the jar in the aquarium and remove the lid. Close the mesh top and let the spider come out of the jar on its own. You can remove the jar once you're sure the spider has moved out. Tape black paper on the outside

> ❝
> *. . . in every **continent** and in nearly every **country** there is the **common** idea—that it is **unlucky** or **unwise** for a man to **kill** a spider.*
> ❞
>
> —W. S. Bristowe, *The World of Spiders*

of one or two of the aquarium walls to make the spider show up well.

3 **FEED AND WATER YOUR SPIDER.**

Food: Provide three to five live insects a week as meals. Each should be about the same weight as the spider. See *Finding Bugs* (p. 7) for ways to catch bugs to feed your spider, OR raise your own houseflies (See Workshop 1), OR feed larger spiders store-bought grasshoppers or crickets, OR raise fruit flies—set out fruit, Jell-O, oatmeal, or honey, and fruit flies should show up. Keep them in a container with a very fine mesh screen on top, and they'll lay eggs and multiply.

Water: Once a week, soak a cotton ball in water and place it on a jar lid

inside the cage. The cotton should be about four times the spider's body size. Never put open water in the cage; spiders drown easily, and small ones can drown in just a drop of water. Spiders don't have tongues to lap up water; your spider will take the cotton in its jaws and suck the water out.

 4 **OBSERVE YOUR SPIDER.** Record what your spiders do,

and when and how they do it. Get to know their daily habits—when and where they weave a web, eat, and rest. Note their response to changes in light, weather, temperature, and humidity. Sketch, photograph, or video your spider in different situations and activities.

WORKSHOP RESOURCE >>
International Society of Arachnology
www.arachnology.org

> In what weather is your spider most active? Most inactive? Why do you think this might be?

CONSIDER THIS!   PRESENT THIS!

> Use excerpts from your observation journal to create a slide show with photographs and narration.

> **GO THE EXTRA MILE!** Observe people's reactions to spiders in your home or science fair. For more, check out Workshop 9, Arachnophobia!

THE EYE OF THE BUTTERFLY

(figure out what color a butterfly favors)

the basics

BUTTERFLIES EAT SWEET NECTAR from flowers for nutrition, and they pollinate the flowers as they do so. Caterpillars (butterfly larvae) eat bitter-tasting plants. Scientists think that this helps them repel predators.

TIME NEEDED >
a weekend (2–3 days)

SCIENCE >
entomology, behavior

SCIENCE CONCEPTS >
vision, behavior modification, color discrimination

ADULT INVOLVEMENT >
It's necessary to boil water to make nectar to feed the butterflies. Kitchen supervision needed!

the buzz

Arizona State University biologist Ron Rutowski studied the vision of butterflies to figure out what they could see, in hopes of discovering how near they needed to be to potential mates to find them. He learned that a butterfly's vision is 20/200—that is, compared to humans with good eyesight who can see details 200 feet away, a butterfly can only see details at 20 feet away. Ron says that if a butterfly were human, it would be legally blind. But butterflies get around. Some species migrate thousands of miles, using the angle of sunlight as a guide.

the QUESTION >>

What color food container does a butterfly prefer? Can you teach butterflies to choose another color?

the PLAN >>

Use different colored feeders to see which color butterflies prefer. Then fill the "unfavorite" feeder with nectar and see if the butterflies will learn to favor it.

the lingo

behavior modification—a system using rewards to change the way an individual behaves

you'll need

3 baby food jars
red, yellow, and white paints
a brush
nectar—Boil four cups of water. Add one cup of sugar. Stir and cool.
hammer
nail
string
butterflies or a butterfly garden

what to do

1 **BUILD THREE NECTAR FEEDERS.** For each feeder, use a baby food jar. Remove the lid and paint the outside of it. Paint one lid bright red, another yellow, and the third white. Use a hammer and nail to poke holes in the lid. Your butterflies will feed through these. Fill the jars to the top with nectar. Screw the lids on tightly, and tie string around the mouths of the jars. Hang the feeders near one another in a tree, from a bird-feeder hook or from a railing, in the area where the butterflies are found. If you're using an inside enclosure, sit the jars at the bottom of the enclosure.

2 **OBSERVE BUTTERFLIES.** Observe the interaction of butterflies and jars. Which jar gets the most visitors?

3 **SWITCH IT UP.** Once you have established which color the butterflies favor, take the feeders down and refill the butterflies' two favorite feeders with plain water and their least favorite feeder with nectar. Then observe your butterflies. How do they behave? Do they change their feeder preference?

4 **ONE MORE TIME.** Try two different methods:
a. Refill all three feeders with nectar. Observe how the butterflies behave.
b. Place just the lids of the jars outside. Observe which one the butterflies visit first.

WORKSHOP RESOURCES >>

The Butterfly Site shows you how to raise butterflies whose eggs you find outside.
http://www.thebutterflysite.com/rearing.shtml

Monarch Watch shows you how to care for butterflies from egg to adult.
http://www.monarchwatch.org/rear/index.htm

Butterfly School gives advice on raising butterflies from caterpillars you find outside.
http://www.butterflyschool.org/teacher/raising.html

> **Butterfly Kits**
The Butterfly and Nature Gift Store
http://www.butterfly-gifts.com/live-butterfly-kits.html

Nature Pavilion
http://www.naturepavilion.com/liveinsectkits.html

> **Where to Get Butterflies**
Raise them: There are commercially available kits for raising your own, OR raise butterflies whose eggs you find outside. There are instructions at the Butterfly Site. See *The Resources* (p. 78).

Convey your data about how many butterfly "hits" each jar got by filling the jars with a candy such as M&M'S or Life Savers, one for each hit. (You might even add to your behavior study by putting out three dishes of small candy that are exactly the same except for their color. Count the candy before the science fair; count it afterward to see which color the humans chose most often!)

CONSIDER THIS! PRESENT THIS!

> Construct a display that includes your three butterfly feeders.

X-RAY VISION

(Photograph the inside of an insect's head)

TIME NEEDED >
two days

SCIENCE >
chemistry, entomology, microscopy

SCIENCE CONCEPTS >
physiology, insect specimen preparation and handling

ADULT INVOLVEMENT >
Chemicals and equipment are involved. Do this experiment in your lab at school, with your teacher nearby. Ask your teacher to handle disposal of materials.

the basics

DEAD INSECTS QUICKLY DRY UP** and disintegrate as water evaporates from their cells and bacteria begins to cause decay. Entomologists who want to study them need to "fix" their bodies with liquid preservative.

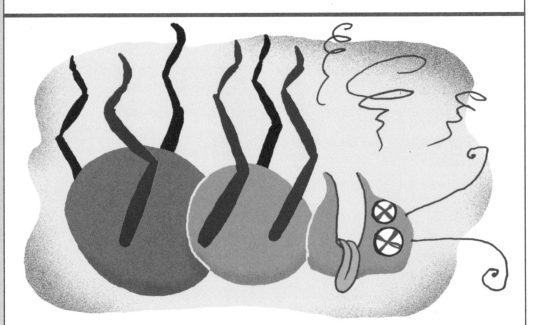

the lingo

collecting—keeping dead insects in order to study, identify, and compare them

you'll need

a microscope—Reserve microscope time at school.

a 35-millimeter camera—digital or film

well slides (microscope slides that have a small indentation in them to hold the insect) **and slide covers**

distilled water

bottle caps

tweezers

an eye dropper

isopropyl alcohol—the highest concentration you can find. Most drugstores sell alcohol in concentrations up to 91 or 95 percent. If you can't find this, a lower percentage will do. (Common rubbing alcohol from the grocery store is usually 70 percent.) **NOTE:** *DO NOT use denatured alcohol. It's poisonous.*

ants or other small insects—The simplest and most humane way to

the QUESTION >> What's inside an insect's head?

the PLAN >> Preserve insects by fixation, prepare specimens, and look inside an insect's head.

kill insects is to put each one in a small plastic bag or jar and place it in the freezer for half an hour or so.

what to do

1 **SET UP YOUR CAMERA** with the microscope. See *Video It* (p. 78).

2 **MAKE YOUR FIXING SOLUTION.** You don't need more than a few milliliters of the solution to make a few slides.

Make a 35 percent solution of alcohol. ***With 91 percent alcohol:*** For example, 91 percent alcohol is already diluted with some water. $91 - 35 = 56$, so you'll use 35 parts of alcohol with 56 parts of distilled water. If you reduce the fraction of 35/56, you can come up with 9/14. That's 9 ml of alcohol and 14 ml of distilled water.

With 70 percent alcohol: $70 - 35 = 35$ parts of distilled water. So use half distilled water, half alcohol.

3 **PLACE THE DEAD INSECT** in a bottle cap and use an eyedropper to add solution to cover the insect. Soak ants and fleas for at least an hour. Bigger bugs may be soaked for up to six hours.

4 **USE TWEEZERS TO TAKE** the insect out of the solution and place it in the well on the slide. Add a drop of solution, and set the slide cover on top.

5 **PLACE YOUR SLIDE UNDER** the microscope, and take a look. Keep a record for each specimen.

6 **PHOTOGRAPH YOUR** specimens on their slides. Be sure to photograph your specimens at low magnification. Then, when you process your pictures, enlarge them, either digitally or in the darkroom. Low magnification provides good depth of field, which helps you identify details in a photograph.

WORKSHOP RESOURCES >>

Science Stuff: www.sciencestuff.com
Lab Warehouse: www.sciplus.com
Experiment source: "Getting Inside an Ant's Head" by Shawn Carlson, "The Amateur Scientist," *Scientific American,* June 1997.

> How might you change your experiment to produce better results? Longer or shorter soaking period? Use a different specimen? Experiment to find out.

CONSIDER THIS! PRESENT THIS!

> Diagram the inside of an insect's head, based on your findings. Add labels to one of your photographs, or do a drawing based on a photograph. Try to orient the diagram so that it matches the angle of the head in your photograph, so that viewers can easily make comparisons.

> **GO THE EXTRA MILE!** Get information about the structures observed inside the ants' and other insects' heads by doing research on the Web or in books.

CATAPULT LEGS

(Demonstrate the properties of a flea's legs)

the basics

FLEAS, LIKE ALL INSECTS, work against air resistance as they move. The flea has a waterproof, lightweight, shock-resistant body that works with an extraordinary leg construction.

TIME NEEDED >
a weekend

SCIENCE >
physics, physiology, mechanics/engineering

SCIENCE CONCEPT >
potential energy

ADULT INVOLVEMENT>
help sawing and drilling materials

the buzz

New research finds that the flea protein that produces resilin may be used to repair damaged arteries in humans. Scientists used this protein to create a superstrong, rubbery polymer that might be used in surgery. They got the protein from a fruit fly and grew it inside *E. coli* bacteria to produce the molecule they needed to make their polymer.

the lingo

elastic—a material that returns to its shape after being bent, squashed, or stretched

polymer—a natural or synthetic compound made up of small simple molecules linked together

you'll need

a jar—for catching and briefly keeping insects (see *Finding Bugs,* p. 7)

a pegboard—two triangles about 12" x 14" x 14." Match up the holes so both pieces are identical. Saw off two points of the triangles for safety.

wood—*catapult arm:* one 1/2" x 1" x 15" piece of wood. Drill eight holes about one inch apart, beginning three inches from one end of the piece and ending four inches from the other end. Use wood glue to attach a small plastic container to one end.

catapult base: one 1/2" x 1 1/2" x 15"

the QUESTION >>

Can a man-made catapult produce a launch of the same ratio as a flea's jump?

the PLAN >>

Make a catapult, a machine that stores energy and focuses it into a throw to make an object accelerate the way a flea's legs accelerate.

A flea's *coxa*—the segment of its leg closest to its body—contains a resilin pad. This springy, elastic pad stores energy as the flea waits to jump. Like a spring pressed down tightly or a rubber band pulled taut, once released the resilin pad expands fast—much faster than the muscles themselves could push. The potential energy of the flea's muscle is stored in the resilin and released as kinetic (moving) energy.

Coxa

piece of wood
one screw eye
one screw hook
six wood screws
two nuts and two 1-3/4" bolts
rubber bands
things to launch—marshmallows, peas, table tennis balls, pinecones, plastic bugs. . .

what to do

1 FIND A JUMPING INSECT.

Look for fleas on a dog or cat. Find grasshoppers, katydids, or crickets outside, or purchase crickets at a pet shop or aquarium shop. They are all great jumpers!

2 MEASURE THE HEIGHT

of your insect, standing; measure the jump of your insect. Do the math: How many times its own height can your insect jump? Compare this to yourself: How many times your height can you jump? How many times your height can you throw? Can you think of ways you could multiply the force of your jump or throw?

NOTE: *Your answers will be a ratio— jump: height. For example, if you are 5 feet tall and you can throw a ball 60 feet, then your jump: height ratio is 60:5, or 12:1.*

3 MAKE A CATAPULT. Follow

the materials instructions (See *You'll Need*, previous page) and this drawing to build the catapult.

- Place the screw eye in the catapult base, one inch from one end. Lay this piece of wood flat.
- Place the screw hook in the catapult arm (smaller piece of wood) on its narrow side, one inch from one end.
- Attach the larger piece of wood to the bases of the triangles.
- Insert one bolt through one triangle, through one hole in the side of the smaller piece of wood, through the other triangle. Attach the nut.
- Insert the other bolt into one triangle and out the other, without passing it through the smaller piece of wood. The bolt should pass under the smaller piece of wood. This will stop the catapult arm after it launches.

Bolt

Nut

Screw
Hook

Rubber
Band

Screw
Eye

Wood Screws

4 **TEST AND IMPROVE YOUR CATAPULT.** Try flinging different objects with your catapult. Measure the objects and the results of your flings by coming up with a ratio, as you did when you measured your bug's leap.

5 **CALCULATE THE DIFFERENCE** between the bug's jumping ratio and your best catapult fling.

WORKSHOP RESOURCE >>

Do an Internet search for information about the grasshopper robot built by scientists Dario Floreano and Mirko Kovac of the Swiss Federal Institute of Technology. It set a high-jump record for a robot.

> Experiment with placing the top bolt through different holes on the catapult arm. Which creates the launching angle that works best? How can you measure the launching angle?

CONSIDER THIS! PRESENT THIS!

> Make a graph that compares different objects fired with the catapult. You may include angle of launch (in degrees), length of flight (in centimeters), and time of flight (in seconds).

> **GO THE EXTRA MILE!** How else could you tweak your catapult's construction or your flinging method to improve your ratio?

Many small insects rely on a kind of catapult mechanism to jump. Using a camera that can take 2,000 pictures a second, Malcolm Burrows of Britain's Cambridge University discovered that the froghopper's catapult is a lot more efficient than the flea's.

—All Things Considered
*National Public Radio,
August 1, 2003*

ARACHNOPHOBIA!

(Design a questionnaire to study spider phobia)

the basics

ARACHNOPHOBIA IS the most common form of animal phobia. Spider fear has been associated with disgust sensitivity (a strong reaction to anything disgusting), negative experiences with spiders, lack of positive or neutral experiences with spiders, parents' expressions of fear or disgust toward spiders, and gender.

TIME NEEDED >
2 or 3 days

SCIENCE >
psychology

SCIENCE CONCEPTS >
testing methods, human behavior and learning

ADULT INVOLVEMENT >
Get permission from parents for kids to participate. Parents may participate, too.

>> Check with your teacher before involving human subjects in your projects.

the buzz

Psychologists are working on ways to help people with arachnophobia. Arachnophobes are often found to have little experience with or knowledge about spiders, so helping them to understand spiders better— and to know what to expect from spiders, such as the fact that a spider won't jump off its web to attack you—can help lessen fear of spiders.

the QUESTION >> Who's afraid of spiders— and why? Can arachnophobes learn to be less afraid?

the PLAN >> You'll question subjects about fear of spiders and try ways to lessen their fear.

the lingo

involuntary responses—elevated heart rate, sweating, shivering
voluntary responses—jumping up, running away, flapping a hand, or squashing a spider

you'll need

a group of willing subjects
a computer with printer or a copier
a spider (see Workshop 5, *Watching Spiders*)
a video of a spider—optional

what to do

1 **WRITE A QUESTIONNAIRE.** Figure out what you want to learn about people's reactions to spiders, and write questions that will help you find out. For example, you might want to know what aspect of spiders your subjects dislike. You could ask these questions:

- Do spiders make you scream or want to run away?
- Would you sleep in a room where a spider has a web?
- What disgusts you most about spiders: (a) the way they move? (b) their legs? (c) their mouths or fangs? (d) being surprised by them? (e) their eating habits?

Consider what you need to know about the people who will answer

> " Which images, if any, are intolerable?
> Which images are tolerable?
> Which images are so nice that you might place them
> in your bedroom? "

—Sample questions from <u>A Spiderless Arachnophobia Therapy:
Comparison Between Placebo and Treatment Groups and
Six-Month Follow-Up Study</u>

*by Laura Carmila Granado, Ronald Ranvaud, and Javier Ropero Peláez,
Neural Plasticity, July 9, 2007*

your questionnaire. Do you want to know their ages? Their gender? Whether they live in a city, town, or rural area? Whether they've ever been bitten by a spider? Think about what might help you understand your group, and write questions to serve that need.

Decide how you will analyze the results of your questionnaire. Write questions that can be answered in a way you can count. Create a scale. For example, subjects might answer 1 to 4:

  1: not at all
  2: a little
  3: some
  4: a lot

2 GIVE YOUR SUBJECTS THE QUESTIONNAIRE.

3 COUNT AND GRAPH YOUR RESPONSES.

4 SEE IF YOU CAN CHANGE PEOPLE'S REACTIONS TO SPIDERS THROUGH A NUMBER OF METHODS.

- Give them a chance to watch a spider in a safe situation for a number of minutes, or for a number of days. (Experiment to find out what is most effective.) Scientists describe this as *in vivo* exposure. It means exposure to a real, live spider. (See Workshop 5, *Watching Spiders*.)

- Give them printed information about spiders, including statistics about spider bites, diseases spread by spiders, and spider behavior, or have them read a website about spiders.
- Have them watch videos of spiders or animations showing spiders. This is called virtual reality exposure.
- Give them a plush toy spider to hold while watching the video or looking at the spider.

After taking these steps to help your subjects get over their fears, give the questionnaire again to see whether their attitudes have changed.

WORKSHOP RESOURCES >>

Do an Internet search to find the Fear of Spiders Questionnaire, the Spider Phobia Questionnaire (SPQ), and the Spider Phobia Questionnaire for Children, designed specifically for children ages 8 to 12.

Source of a Spider Video
http://news.nationalgeographic.com/news/2006/02/0214_060214_spider_video.html

You might want to know about the effect parents have on their kids' fears. Write questions for both kids and parents that ask them about their opinions of spiders. But also ask the kids about their experiences with spiders, what their parents have told them about them, and where they think their attitudes toward spiders come from. Ask the parents what they have told their kids about spiders, how they handle finding a spider in the house, and where their own attitudes toward spiders come from.

CONSIDER THIS! PRESENT THIS!

Present the arachnophobes you worked with as case studies. Include photos and quotes; interview each subject to find out whether his or her arachnophobia was affected by the experience you provided.

GO THE EXTRA MILE! Keep your project going in real time by observing the reactions of people to your display!

ROLY-POLY MAZE

(Teach pill bugs by using their instinct to stay out of the light)

the basics

PILL BUGS ARE NOT INSECTS. They are terrestrial (land-dwelling) crustaceans related to lobsters, shrimp, and crayfish. They have modified gills called pseudotrachea that allow them to breathe in the water or in the damp—but they must stay damp to keep breathing. They live in dark places such as the undersides of stones, logs, and piles of leaves.

TIME NEEDED ›
one to two days

SCIENCE ›
bug behavior, psychology

SCIENCE CONCEPT ›
phototaxis

ADULT INVOLVEMENT ›
help with the hot glue gun

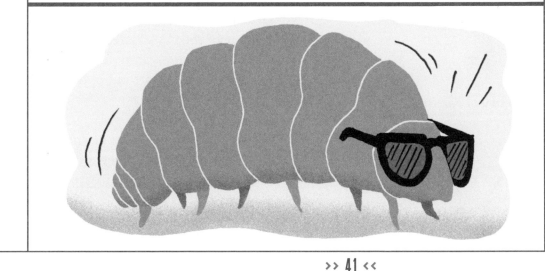

the buzz

Pill bugs are decomposers. They eat rotting plants after they fall to the ground. Lester Ehler, a California entomologist, figured out that pill bugs climb healthy plants to eat the eggs of stinkbugs—pests that eat crops. Ehler recommends that farmers plant plants that pill bugs like at the edges of their fields, instead of spraying pesticides to kill stinkbugs.

the QUESTION >> Can a pill bug learn to find its way through a maze?

the PLAN >> Use light to train pill bugs to find their way through a maze.

"
Pill bugs can also make great pets!
"

—University of Kentucky
Department of Entomology website

the lingo

phototaxis—the phenomenon by which insects (and other organisms) are guided by light. Crickets and pill bugs run to the cover of darkness; moths and june bugs are drawn to light. When pill bugs dash for the shelter of a dark rock, it's an example of negative phototaxis. When moths fly toward the porch light, it's positive phototaxis.

you'll need

pill bugs—It's a good idea to try training several bugs at once. That way you can compare them, and if one dies, your experiment doesn't die with it.

a maze—made of these objects:
» a clear plastic box, a sandwich container, or a small pan
» thick corrugated cardboard
» a hot glue gun and glue sticks
» a crayon

two flashlights

an obstacle—something to block the passage of the bug. Find an object that slides squarely into the passage, or make a closing gate out of cardboard. There should be no room for the bug to get through.

pill bug house—Each pill bug should have its own house. Collect coffee cans. Punch holes in each plastic lid. Fill the can with the most decayed leaves you can find; get them when

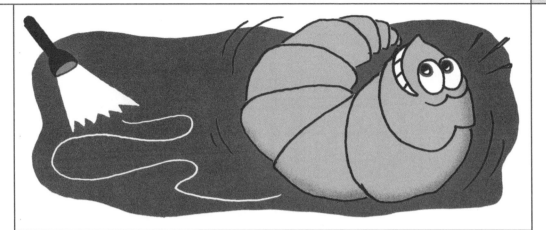

they're almost turned to dirt. Mix the leaves with a little sand, and then fill the cans about halfway. Add a pill bug, a piece of raw potato (peeled), and a piece of damp sponge to every can. You'll need to keep the sponges damp and replace the potatoes every two or three days.

what to do

1 FIND PILL BUGS. Look under a stone, log, or pile of damp leaves. You can also set a trap for them. Here's how: Cut a potato in half, and hollow it out. Place the potato, flat side down, outside in a quiet area. Cover it with leaves or grass. It should attract pill bugs in one or two days.

2 MAKE THE MAZE. Use the cardboard to make a T-shaped run inside the box:
- Draw the T-shaped run, using a ruler and your crayon.
- Cut cardboard strips about an inch wide.
- Cut these strips to fit the lines you made with the crayon. Bend the cardboard at the corners of the T, rather than having strips meet there. Let strips meet on the straightaways, overlapping them slightly so there are no openings in the wall.
- Hot-glue the strips into the bottom of the box, following the crayon lines.

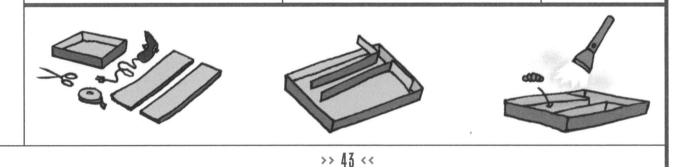

3 CONDUCT YOUR EXPERIMENT:

A. Place the pill bug in the bottom of the T. Shine the flashlight into the bottom of the T. The bug should crawl toward the top of the T. Watch which way it turns when it reaches the crossbar of the T—right or left. It's important to know this. It determines which way you will try to teach it to turn.

B. When the bug reaches the cross-bar, it will turn left or right. If

it naturally turned right you'll want to teach it to turn left, and vice versa.

C. Scoop up the bug and return it to the start of the T.

D. Shine a flashlight on it when it goes the wrong way.

E. Repeat the training session, up to ten times a day per bug, for three to ten days. You can return each bug to its coffee can (one bug per can!) between maze runs.

F. Keep a careful record of what happens on each run.

WORKSHOP RESOURCE >>

University of Kentucky College of Agriculture Entomology Department, Pill Bug page

http://www.ca.uky.edu/entomology/entfacts/ef439.asp

Experiment adapted from "How to Study Learning in the Sow Bug and Photograph Tiny Live Crustaceans" by C. L. Strong, "The Amateur Scientist," *Scientific American*, May 1967. Note that Strong adapted the experiment of John Frost, a graduate student at California State College at Fullerton.

Why do pill bugs prefer the dark?

CONSIDER THIS! PRESENT THIS!

Make a graph that shows each practice run. This will help you see patterns that develop.

	Run 1	Run 2	Run 3	Run 4	Run 5	Run 6	Run 7
Day 1							
TUCKER	●	●	●	●	●	●	●
ROLO	●	●	●	●	●	●	●
PHIL	●	●	●	●	●	●	●
Correct Turn:	● YES	● NO					

GO THE EXTRA MILE! Play a recording of the song "Roly Poly" at your science fair station for a sure hit. There are versions by Hank Williams, Chuck Berry, Roy Blount, Jr., and the Little Willies.

COMPOSTING: BEYOND WORMS!

(Get inside a compost heap)

the basics

TINY ORGANISMS eat decaying materials, and their metabolisms make the compost pile heat up. The most common invertebrates found in compost are mites, springtails, and nematodes. Earthworms tunnel through the compost, let air through the decaying matter, and poop, which turns compost to rich, dark humus, the key to healthy soil.

TIME NEEDED >
one day to one week with an existing compost heap; you can also create your own compost heap over several months

SCIENCE >
organic chemistry, microbiology

SCIENCE CONCEPT >
decomposition

ADULT INVOLVEMENT >
permission and some assistance in accessing compost heaps

the buzz

Soil ecologist Diana H. Wall of Colorado State University leads the Global Litter Invertebrate Decomposition Experiment (GLIDE). Her team sent bags of alfalfa grass to ecologists in 20 countries. The grass was placed in ecosystems as diverse as the American plains and the African desert and was left alone to decay. A few months later, the team collected the samples and analyzed them. They found thousands of species of decomposers. Scientists are studying the results to figure out how to help improve soil in less fertile lands.

the QUESTION >>

What is the bug activity at different levels in a compost heap? Why are the levels different?

the PLAN >>

Examine samples from different levels in a compost heap.

the lingo

metabolism—the process by which an organism turns food into energy

you'll need

compost heaps—Ask your neighbors and friends for permission to sample their heaps.
a compost thermometer—available at garden supply stores
a yardstick
coffee cans, Styrofoam coffee cups, or other containers with lids—at least three per compost heap
pie tins or cake pans—something wide, with sides, so you can spread compost out to see what lives there
funnel and desk lamp—for capturing and isolating small bugs
tweezers, popsicle sticks, or spoons—something to help you sift through the compost to find and remove the larger bugs
clear jars, small glasses, or plastic dishes—to hold organisms while you look at them under a magnification dissecting microscope or magnifying glass

what to do

1 FIND ONE TO THREE COMPOST HEAPS AND ASK FOR PERMISSION TO STUDY THEM.

2 DESCRIBE AND COMPARE THE CONDITIONS IN THE COMPOST HEAPS. Ask each composter his or her procedure for setting up the compost heap. Take note of details, including the container, the materials placed in the compost, and the length of time since the compost was begun. Ask the composter to describe the heap: Has it heated up? Has it cooled down? Is there a cycle of heating and cooling?

TAKE THESE MEASURE-MENTS FOR EACH COMPOST HEAP:
- temperature outside the compost
- temperature inside the compost
- size of container (measurements)

4 TAKE SAMPLES OF THE COMPOST MATERIAL— enough to fill a coffee can or other container—at different levels of the heap. Label them with their measurement (how far from the bottom of the heap, or how far from the edge of the heap).

5 ANALYZE THE COMPOST MATERIAL. Separate, study, and identify each organism you find.
- Use the cake pans or pie tins to spread material out. With a spoon or tweezer, gently remove large insects, and place them in small glass dishes or coffee cans. Remember to note where the organisms came from!
- Once larger bugs have been removed, place a handful of compost in the cup of a small funnel. Place a clear jar, half full of water, beneath the funnel, and direct a desk lamp toward the top of the funnel. Small organisms will crawl down, away from the light and heat, and drop into the water.

 WORKSHOP RESOURCE >>
Cornell University suggests several ways to create your

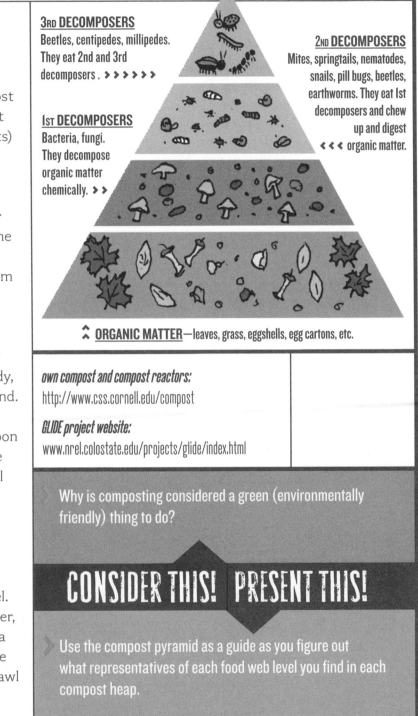

3RD DECOMPOSERS
Beetles, centipedes, millipedes. They eat 2nd and 3rd decomposers . >>>>>>

2ND DECOMPOSERS
Mites, springtails, nematodes, snails, pill bugs, beetles, earthworms. They eat 1st decomposers and chew up and digest <<< organic matter.

1ST DECOMPOSERS
Bacteria, fungi. They decompose organic matter chemically. >>

ORGANIC MATTER—leaves, grass, eggshells, egg cartons, etc.

own compost and compost reactors:
http://www.css.cornell.edu/compost

GLIDE project website:
www.nrel.colostate.edu/projects/glide/index.html

Why is composting considered a green (environmentally friendly) thing to do?

CONSIDER THIS! PRESENT THIS!

> Use the compost pyramid as a guide as you figure out what representatives of each food web level you find in each compost heap.

> GO THE EXTRA MILE! Look at the compost through a microscope to find the smallest organisms, which will include tiny bacteria and different types of fungi.

I'VE GOT WORMS!

(Find the reproduction rate of compost worms)

TIME NEEDED >
two to three months
(or you can calculate
results)

SCIENCE >
biology, physiology

SCIENCE CONCEPTS >
decomposition,
compost, reproduction

the basics

USUALLY COMPOSTING WORMS can process (eat and poop) an amount equal to their weight every day. Under certain conditions they may process several times their weight. But how quickly they mate and reproduce also depends on the conditions.

the buzz

Is the ability of earthworms to reproduce related to the nutritional quality of their compost heap? One worm grower found that 25 worms produced 150 eggs and 250 hatchlings over two weeks. For each adult, the most eggs expected per week is 3.8 (an average), with 3.3 hatchlings surviving per egg. So the rate of reproduction for adults worms is more than ten per week per adult.

the lingo

cocoon—For worms, *cocoon* is another word for egg. For insects, a cocoon is a capsule spun around the immature insect during metamorphosis to the adult form.

you'll need

composting worms—red worms (*Eisenia fetida*—also known as red wigglers) or European nightcrawlers (*Eisenia hortensis*). Buy at a pet store or compost supply. You don't need many; a pound of composting worms may have a thousand individuals. Just don't dig them up in the backyard. Backyard worms won't live in a worm bin!

NOTE: You don't need to worry about including enough males and females. Worms have the sexual organs of both males and females and can mate with any other individual. All worms will lay eggs.

a three-gallon plastic storage container—opaque (nontransparent) with a lid with four or five holes drilled in the top and sides for air, and three holes in the bottom for drainage (use a 1/8" drill bit). You can also use a blue recycling bin with a lid. Put an extra lid underneath to catch worm tea (pee).
infrared lamp
bedding materials—Brown card-

the QUESTION >> What is the rate of reproduction of my worms?

the PLAN >> Raise red worms and observe their reproduction, growth, and composting ability.

board and rotting leaves are best; you could also include paper, straw, coconut husk, peat moss, or a combination of several of these items.
compost materials for worm food—vegetable and fruit peelings, cores, old fruit, used paper towels, shredded newspaper, tea bags, coffee grounds (you can collect these in a can in your kitchen and transfer them to your worm bin once a day)

what to do

1 **SET UP YOUR WORM BIN.**
After drilling the holes in your bin, fill it one-third to halfway with bedding. Your worm bin must have:
- **food:** Worms eat the microorganisms that feed on the compost materials.
- **darkness:** Daylight can be harmful to these worms; use an infrared light when you look at them, but mostly keep the lid on and the darkness in.
- **air:** You can assure a good oxygen level by using the right kind of bedding—shreds of cardboard,

leaves, and a variety of papers.

- **warmth:** Keep the bin in an area where the temperature is between 55 and 70ºF. Although worms can survive in different conditions, this temperature range is best for breeding.
- **moisture:** The material in your bin should be kept damp. Worm experts say it should feel like a sponge that has been squeezed out—wetter than a typical compost heap, but not soggy, soupy, or wet.

2 **AFTER TEN DAYS TO TWO WEEKS, YOU SHOULD BE ABLE TO FIND COCOONS IN YOUR BEDDING MATERIAL.** Gently turn over the material in your bin to find them. They look like small, shiny, round lemons shaded from pale yel-low to black. (The blacker it is, the more close the cocoon is to hatching.) Each cocoon holds about 20 young, but only 3 or 4 will survive.

3 **CALCULATE THE REPRODUCTION RATE.** The reproduction time from mating to hatching ranges from a month to ten weeks. But you can count cocoons and estimate that 3.3 hatchlings from each cocoon will survive to adulthood. Multiply the number of cocoons by 3.3 to figure the total reproduction level of your worm bin. Divide that total by the number of worms you started with to find the reproduction rate per worm.

4 **REMOVE CASTINGS (POOP).** Experts suggest placing food in the bin at one end to train the worms to go that way. This allows you to remove bedding from the other end in order to exchange some used material for unused material. If you scoop out a few worms in the process, put them back in.

WORKSHOP RESOURCES >>

"Making a Worm Farm," Louisiana Department of Environmental Quality:
http://www.deq.louisiana.gov/portal/tabid/2101/Default.aspx

Smithsonian Institution Department of Invertebrate Zoology Worm Page:
http://invertebrates.si.edu/worms.htm

Do you think running a worm farm would be a good business for you?

CONSIDER THIS!   PRESENT THIS!

Encourage visitors to your science fair table to adopt a worm. Let them fill out a form giving the worm a name, and post the names.

GO THE EXTRA MILE! Some growers think adding crushed egg shells to your bedding material makes the worms reproduce faster. Experiment to find out.

FOOD FACTORY

(Learn about the business of raising insects for insect-eating reptiles)

the basics

NSECT-EATING REPTILES include lizards, chameleons, snakes, and turtles. They eat crickets and mealworms, as well as other arthropods such as brine shrimp.

TIME NEEDED ›
two or three days

SCIENCE ›
economics, agriculture

SCIENCE CONCEPTS ›
food chain, nutrition, economics of the bug farm

ADULT INVOLVEMENT ›
transportation and/or assistance with phone calls

>> *This project involves business plans; you may also need to raise insects as an experiment to meet your science fair requirements. Ask your teacher.*

the buzz

There are about a million people working in insect fields in the United States. Gary Hevel, entomologist and public information officer at the Smithsonian Institution Museum of Natural History, divides the workers up this way:

- **nozzleheads:** people working on controlling insects in agriculture. Their work involves researching, testing, and using ways to keep insects under control among plants, especially crops.
- **pest controllers:** people working on controlling insects in other environments where they might affect people or property or spread disease
- **entomologists:** people working to identify insects, assess populations, and establish relationships between insects

the lingo

food chain—consumers and the food they eat or prey upon

consumers—eaters in the food chain

you'll need

a calculator
information—about the life cycle of your bug and costs associated with it (available from pet stores and online)
optional—aquarium and other equipment needed for keeping insects (see *Keeping Bugs*, p. 8)

what to do

Research and complete this list of questions and calculations.

the QUESTION >> What's the best way for the owner of a pet reptile to be supplied with live insects for food—to buy insects or to grow them?

the PLAN >> Compare the cost of buying worms or crickets in a store with raising your own, and with raising enough surplus insects to sell to others.

1 WORM COST/STORE-BOUGHT:

- How many mealworms does the average turtle, lizard, or snake eat over a certain time period?
- How much do those worms cost in the store?
- How much will worms cost per year if you buy them in the store?

2 WORM COST/HOME-GROWN:

- In order to provide that many mealworms on a regular basis for your pet, how many worms would have to be mature and ready for chomping at any given time?

- How would you set up a worm farm that would provide you with the right number of worms when you need them?
- How many eggs do you have to buy now to get started?
- How many eggs do you have to buy in the future?

(In other words, how many different stages do you need to keep your worms at in order to ensure the right supply when your pet needs them? How long is it going to take before you have a bunch of them at different stages, and they are perpetuating themselves?)

- How much it is going to cost you to get to this level? What will you need to spend on eggs, worms, containers, worm food, and other items?

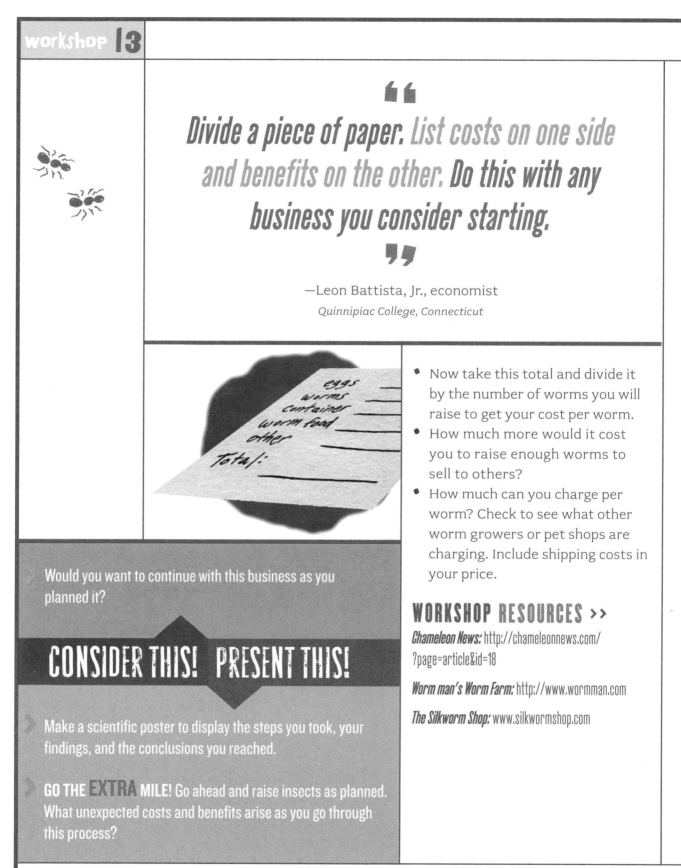

> **Divide a piece of paper.** List costs on one side and benefits on the other. **Do this with any business you consider starting.**

—Leon Battista, Jr., economist
Quinnipiac College, Connecticut

- Now take this total and divide it by the number of worms you will raise to get your cost per worm.
- How much more would it cost you to raise enough worms to sell to others?
- How much can you charge per worm? Check to see what other worm growers or pet shops are charging. Include shipping costs in your price.

WORKSHOP RESOURCES >>

Chameleon News: http://chameleonnews.com/?page=article&id=18

Worm man's Worm Farm: http://www.wormman.com

The Silkworm Shop: www.silkwormshop.com

Would you want to continue with this business as you planned it?

CONSIDER THIS!   PRESENT THIS!

Make a scientific poster to display the steps you took, your findings, and the conclusions you reached.

GO THE EXTRA MILE! Go ahead and raise insects as planned. What unexpected costs and benefits arise as you go through this process?

EATING UP THE ROAD

(Investigate ant tunnels)

the basics

ANTS DON'T DIG THEIR TUNNELS with their legs. Instead, they chew through sand and dirt to make tunnels, walkways, and secret chambers in a very purposeful way.

TIME NEEDED >
two days to a week

SCIENCE >
biology, entomology, behavior

SCIENCE CONCEPTS >
ant habitat and nutrition, science in orbit

ADULT INVOLVEMENT >

the buzz

Fowler High School students Rachel Poppe, Abby Golash, Brad Miller, and Liban Muhamed, of Syracuse, New York, sent an experiment on the space shuttle *Columbia*, hoping to find out if being in space would affect how ants make tunnels. The ants became more active than they had been on Earth, but the ants' space tunnels didn't seem to take the purposeful paths they usually did. The students intended to analyze the ants' habitat when *Columbia* returned to Earth, but their ants met a sad end. *Columbia* is the space shuttle that disintegrated upon reentry to Earth's atmosphere, destroying the ship and killing every living thing on board, including its crew.

the lingo

agar—a gel made from seaweed. It is a source of sugars and amino acids that ants usually get from eating other bugs or seeds. Using agar as a medium in which ants can build tunnels and live without other kinds of food has revolutionized the business of ant farms.

you'll need

four containers—tall drinking glasses, clear-sided plastic boxes, or petri dishes

lids—mesh or old nylon stockings and rubber bands for the glasses, or petri dish lids with perforations

agar gel—recipe below

food coloring (optional)

food supplements—60 milliliters of honey, sugar, maple syrup, fruit juice, vitamin water, gatorade, yeast, bouillon, or Ovaltine

8 to 12 ants—Harvester ants were used in the space shuttle experiment because of their strength and hardiness, but you can use any ants that you find. For help finding ants, see *Finding Bugs* (p. 7) or Workshop 13.

Agar Gel Recipe
Ingredients:
    500 ml water
    1 egg
    5 grams agar (available from science supply or health food stores)
Directions:
1. Set half the water (250 ml) aside.
2. Mix the other half (250 ml) of the water with the egg. Use a fork or mixer. If you want colored agar,

QUESTION >> How do ants behave in different tunneling materials?

PLAN >> Create and compare ant habitats to see how well the ants do with different food supplements combined with agar.

add a drop of food coloring.

3. Mix the two water portions together.

4. Add the agar and mix until smooth.

5. Pour the same amount into each of the glasses, about half the height of the container.

6. Add a different food supplement to each glass.

7. Store in the refrigerator until the mixture sets like Jell-O.

what to do

1 ADD TWO OR THREE ANTS TO EACH CONTAINER. Use a drinking straw. Place one end over the ant, and put your thumb over the other end. This creates a vacuum in the straw strong enough to lift the ant. Keeping your thumb on the straw end and one hand under (but not touching) the ant, transport the ant to the glass. You can use the straw to make a few holes in the medium to get the ant started.

2 OBSERVE YOUR ANTS FOR TWO DAYS TO A WEEK. What do they do? What do they eat? How active are they? Take careful notes on their behavior. Which supplement seems best for the ants? Which ants have the most energy and greatest activity level?

WORKSHOP RESOURCES >:

Source of AntWorks Ant Farm with Blue Gel: Discovery Channel Stores; Fat Brain Toys, http://www.fatbraintoys.com; and Target stores

Source of Uncle Milton's Ant Farm: http://www.unclemilton.com

Source of AntQuarium with Pink Gel: www.toydirectory.com

A homeschooler who studied AntWorks found that the ants brought dead bodies to the surface of the gel. What do your ants do if one of them dies?

CONSIDER THIS! PRESENT THIS!

Fill an aquarium or other clear container with the substance that proved most successful for your ants, and move the ants there. Lit from behind, your ant farm makes a beautiful—and informative—display.

GO THE EXTRA MILE! How does the ants' use of agar compare with their natural medium of sand or dirt?

CRICKET- & MOTH- EATEN SOCKS

(Compare bugs' eating habits)

TIME NEEDED >
one day to one month

SCIENCE >
entomology, behavior,
nutrition

SCIENCE CONCEPT >
diet and behavior of
insects

ADULT INVOLVEMENT >
Ask a parent/guardian
about the best location
for this experiment.
Consider an area away
from living space.

the basics

SEVERAL DIFFERENT SPECIES of clothing moths lay their eggs in wool. If you see silk threads or small droppings in a piece of wool—not to mention holes—you've got clothing moths. Other noted wool eaters include carpet beetles and crickets.

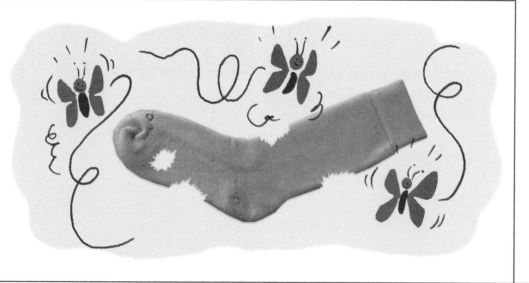

the buzz

Experts say that adult moths don't eat wool; rather, females lay eggs in the wool, and the larvae that hatch eat the wool. You can identify the cocoons, which are shaped like tiny cigars, in the folds of wool. Note that it can take eggs as long as a month to hatch. But you may find that other bugs also have an interest in wool.

the lingo

omnivore—eats everything
carnivore—eats meat
herbivore—eats plant matter

you'll need

bugs—crickets, katydids, different moths, mealworms or mealmoths, ladybugs, ants (see *Finding Bugs,* p. 7)
old wool clothing—A sweater, jacket, skirt, or pants, cut into pieces roughly 12 inches square. Consider using a dirty, old sweater, or one that has been worn a lot recently. You can also test raw wool that you get from a sheep farm or a knitting store, wool yarn, and other fabrics such as cotton and polyester.

what to do

If you have a month:

1 **SET A FIBER TRAP AND SEE IF BUGS FIND YOUR BAIT.** Place your fabric or fiber samples—clean and dirty wool, raw wool, yarns, and/or other fabrics—in an area that is likely to attract bugs, such as a garage or basement. Place the materials in open areas on or near the ground.

- Every three days, take notes on whether anything seems to have gotten into your materials.
- At the end of the observation period, examine the materials with a magnifying lens or microscope. What evidence of a bug invasion can you find?

the QUESTION >> Which insects are most likely to eat clothing?

the PLAN >> Compare the eating habits of insects, using raw wool, wool yarn, wool fabric, or other fibers.

> **I had a wool moth larva eat through self-patterning sock yarn and you could kind of see the pattern show up in the (egg) case.**

—Kathryn,
a knitter from Seattle, WA

What's the best way to prevent your woolens from getting eaten?

CONSIDER THIS! PRESENT THIS!

Display photographs of materials that have been eaten or colonized by bugs, and include explanations of what sort of behaviors you observed.

GO THE EXTRA MILE! If you've found a material that bugs like eating, consider rubbing a patch of it with lavender, cedar, mothballs, or other bug-repellent materials to test their effectiveness. Does it repel the bug, or does it have no effect?

If you have a day:

2 FIND DIFFERENT BUGS AND SEE WHETHER THEY SHOW INTEREST IN EATING THE MATERIALS YOU PROVIDE. Place one bug at a time in an aquarium or other container that allows you to watch it and gives it plenty of air. Lay out your assortment of materials. Give each bug 30 minutes. Observe the reaction of each different kind of bug to your materials before removing it and giving another bug a chance.

If you have a day and a night:

3 CREATE A SEPARATE SPACE FOR EACH BUG. Leave each bug overnight with its little assortment of materials. In the morning, note what has been bitten or eaten.

WORKSHOP RESOURCE >>
University of California Integrated Pest Management Website on the Moth's Life Cycle
http://www.ipm.ucdavis.edu/PMG/PESTNOTES/pn7435.html

STRIDING ON WATER

(Analyze how water striders stay afloat)

the basics

IN THE MIDDLE OF A BODY OF WATER, a drop of water is round. But when water meets air, gravity pulls the round drop flat, stretching it and creating a layer that is like skin to a tiny bug. Water striders that skim the top of the water make use of this surface tension, balancing their speed and lift to stay afloat. Like a water skier who lets go of the rope, the water strider would sink if it stopped moving.

TIME NEEDED >
one or two days

SCIENCE >
physics, entomology

SCIENCE CONCEPTS >
surface tension,
movement dynamics

ADULT INVOLVEMENT >
NEEDED! This experiment
uses small amounts
of sodium hydroxide,
which can burn if it gets
on your skin. You may
need financial support
for the thymol blue. Do
this experiment in your
school lab with your
teacher nearby, and ask
your teacher to handle
disposal of materials.

the buzz

When David Hu and Brian Chan were graduate students at the Massachusetts Institute of Technology (MIT), they built a water strider robot ten times bigger than the real bug. "It's lightweight, it's supported by surface tension, and it generates vortices." Scientists at Carnegie Mellon University are adapting it. "They want to use water strider robots to clear oil spills in the ocean," says Hu, now a mathematician studying biomechanics at New York University. This workshop is one of his experiments.

the lingo

vortex—liquid forced into a whirlpool (plural: vortices)
biomechanics—the science of muscular activity

you'll need

a baking dish—clear glass
a light table or light box—the kind photographers use to look at slides. If you have a glass-top table, you can place a lamp underneath it, with a sheet of plain paper on top of the glass to diffuse the light.
thymol blue—a coloring chemical*
sodium hydroxide*
NOTE: Be extremely careful using sodium hydroxide (lye). Have an adult present when you use it.
an eyedropper
water strider(s)
a small net
a covered container—to transport the water strider(s)
a camera (optional)
* See *Workshop Resources*, p. 63.

the QUESTION >> How does a water strider stay on the surface of the water?

the PLAN >> View the motions of a water strider to understand biomechanics and surface tension.

what to do

1 **FIND WATER STRIDERS.** You can find them in ponds

or streams. Catch one or two with a little net, and transport them in a cup with just a drop or two of water. It's easy for water striders to drown if they get wet.

2 **PLACE THE BAKING DISH** on the paper above the light with just enough water to cover the bottom. Add three to four drops of sodium hydroxide, then three to four drops of the thymol blue.

3 **ADD THE WATER STRIDER** ten seconds after adding the thymol blue. Use your net and let the strider out gently so it stays on the surface and doesn't get wet.

4 **YOU'LL HAVE ONE MINUTE** to observe the insect's movement across the water—and to photograph it—before the dye sinks. At that point, net the water strider and take it out of the water.

5 **TO REPEAT,** shake the dish to bring the dye to the surface again. Don't do this with the water strider in the water! Do not repeat

this experiment more than three times in order not to unduly stress the water strider.

WORKSHOP RESOURCES >>

To Buy Thymol Blue:
Basic Science Supplies: http://www.basicsciencesupplies.com

To Buy Sodium Hydroxide:
Snowdrift Farm: http://www.snowdriftfarm.com/dry.html

> Does the dye or sodium hydroxide harm the insect? David Hu says no, because water striders are covered in hairs that keep water from getting to their bodies. They have the greatest hair density (number of hairs per skin area) of any animal in the animal kingdom.

CONSIDER THIS! PRESENT THIS!

> Take photographs of the designs your water striders make.

> **GO THE EXTRA MILE!** Look for David Hu's website—and pictures of his water striders—by typing robot strider MIT into any Internet search tool.

SOUNDS BUGGY

(Evaluate insect calls)

TIME NEEDED >
a few days to a week

SCIENCE >
acoustics, physics,
insect physiology and
behavior

SCIENCE CONCEPT >
insect calls

ADULT INVOLVEMENT>
Ask someone to help you
keep an eye on the desk
lamp in the closet.

the basics

INSECTS MAKE LOTS OF NOISES. They may be calling for mates, simply yelling "I'm here," or communicating with each other about food. They also communicate through vibrations, colors, and light.

the buzz

University of Missouri-Columbia biologist Rex Cocroft was a musician before he became a scientist who studies how insects communicate—through vibrations that travel through the leaves and stems of plants the insects are sitting on. These vibrations, unlike the "songs" (called stridulations) of crickets or katydids, are inaudible to humans. Cocroft now researches native Missouri bugs called treehoppers, which live in groups of about 50 and communicate in order to tell each other about new crops of leaves.

the lingo

inaudible—impossible to hear

you'll need

With insects you can hear outside:
outdoor thermometer
phone/Internet access—to call a weather station
camera, sound recorder (optional)

With captive crickets in the house:
crickets
cricket house—See *Keeping Bugs*, p. 8.

the QUESTION >> When and why do insects make the most noise?

the PLAN >> Assess and analyze the calling habits of insects that you hear outside and/or keep captive.

what to do

1 **OBSERVE THE CRICKETS' BEHAVIOR FOR A DAY OR TWO.** Notice when they are chirping and when they are silent. Note the time of day as well as the level of light—full sun, overcast, and so on.

2 **TRY TO COUNT HOW MANY INDIVIDUALS YOU CAN HEAR.** (You may hear things differently after step 3.)

3 **FIGURE OUT WHAT INSECTS ARE MAKING THE NOISE.** Try to find and observe them by catching them briefly. Photograph them.

> "Entomologists (people who study insects) call the way grasshoppers make noise stridulation. . . . Grasshoppers rub two body parts together to make noise. This is kind of like playing a violin."

—Kurt Milton Pickett

Graduate student, Department of Entomology, Ohio State University, Museum of Biological Diversity

Use a desk lamp to lengthen the "day" for your captive crickets. Before sundown, turn on the light and leave it on for an hour or two after the sun sets. Observe (from outside the door) the rate of chirping of your crickets every five minutes during that time. Compare it with the crickets' usual behavior at this time.

CONSIDER THIS! PRESENT THIS!

Make a model of the insects. Show the parts of their bodies that create the noise.

GO THE EXTRA MILE! Play a recording of your cricket sounds to accompany your presentation.

4 **NOTE THE ENVIRONMENTAL CONDITIONS**—such as season, temperature, humidity, dewpoint level (available at a local weather service or online weather Web page), wind, weather conditions, and time of day—at the points when insect noises peak or drop.

WORKSHOP RESOURCE >>
Recordings of Insect Sounds
Nature Songs: http://www.naturesongs.com/insects.html

STRONG AS SILK

(Test the strength of fibers)

the basics

WHAT MAKES A HIGH-PERFORMANCE FIBER? Scientists consider four factors: strength-to-weight ratio (how much they can hold relative to their weight), resistance to flame, resistance to chemicals, and tensile strength (their ability to hold against resistance, lift a weight, or withstand an impact).

TIME NEEDED >
one day

SCIENCE >
biochemistry,
entomology,
textile engineering

SCIENCE CONCEPT >
fiber strength and
weight

ADULT INVOLVEMENT>
none

the buzz

Scientists are using spider silk to create nanofibers—laboratory-made polymers that are extraordinarily strong. Although man-made fibers have taken over the toughest jobs—forming the basis of materials used in airbags for the *Mars Pathfinder*, parachutes for spaceships, racing sails for sailboats, bulletproof vests, even a triathlon bicycle—cell by cell silk made by spiders is still stronger than any man-made material.

the QUESTION >> How does the tensile strength of silk made by silkworms compare with that of other fibers?

the PLAN >> Compare the tensile strengths of different fibers, including silk, cotton, wool, and polyester.

the lingo

polymer—a natural or synthetic compound made up of small, simple molecules linked together in long chains of repeating units

you'll need

a method for testing tensile strength—One way is to use a machine called the Tensile Tester. Where would you find such a machine? Your school might have one in its lab, or a local scientific business might have one you could borrow, either by conducting your experiment in their lab or by bringing the Tensile Tester to your house or school.

You can also use:
a doorway or basement rafter
duct tape or screw-in steel eyelets
a small bucket—with a handle
sand
a scale—kitchen or laboratory
fibers—silk thread, cotton thread, polyester thread, wool yarn, raffia—anything you want to compare. Consider comparing natural and man-made fibers, as well as raw versus processed fibers (such as raw wool versus wool yarn).

what to do

1 GET YOUR EMPTY BUCKET AND WEIGH IT.

2 CUT A 24-INCH STRAND OF EACH FIBER. Attach the top three inches of the strand to the rafter or doorway and the bottom three inches to the handle of the bucket. To be accurate you have to attach each fiber in the same way to the top of the doorway or rafter. For example, if you knot or tape it, be sure to do it in the same way for each fiber.

3 ADD SAND TO THE BUCKET LITTLE BY LITTLE TO MAKE THE FIBER STRETCH. Measure how far each strand stretches before the fiber breaks. (It doesn't count if your knot or tape comes undone; the fiber must stretch to the breaking point.)

4 WHEN THE FIBER BREAKS, WEIGH THE BUCKET AND SAND. Subtract the weight of the bucket to get the weight of sand needed to break this fiber.

NOTE: Your doorway or rafter experiment will result in a weight measurement. Measure this weight in grams; scientists use the metric system. The tensile strength you get from the Tensile Tester will use a standard of measurement called pascals.

WORKSHOP RESOURCE >>

The Mooring and Rigging Group at Woods Hole Oceanographic Institution has a horizontal tensile machine to test every fiber it puts on its ships, submarines, and moorings.
To see it, type Woods Hole tensile into a search bar and look for www.whoi.edu.

> ## If we compare spider dragline silk to Kevlar, we find that the silk has lower strength and stiffness, but ten times greater toughness.

—Christopher Viney, Paul Yager, and Kimberly Carlson, *from the project description for the Silk Protein Project conducted at the University of Washington in Seattle*

Why would spider silk need to be stronger than, say, human hair?

CONSIDER THIS! PRESENT THIS!

> Show a video of fiber-making insects. Search the Internet for videos of insects spinning silk, webs, and cocoons.

> **GO THE EXTRA MILE!** Are you good at knitting, crocheting, braiding, or weaving? Compare the tensile strengths of multiple joined strands of the same fiber.

HOW TO FLY

(Build an insect-size airplane)

TIME NEEDED ›
one weekend

SCIENCE ›
bug physiology,
aerodynamics,
engineering

SCIENCE CONCEPT ›
flight

ADULT INVOLVEMENT ›
needed if you use a
sharp knife to cut
materials

the basics

PEOPLE CLAIM THAT INSECTS shouldn't be able to fly based on the laws of conventional aerodynamics. That's because they're looking at a fixed-wing model of flight. But insects don't have fixed wings. Their wings flap. So how do they fly? By a different set of aerodynamic laws that take into account the relationship of a small body to the force of the air.

the buzz

Z. Jane Wang, a physicist at Cornell University, gets support for her research on dragonfly flight from the military, which hopes to find a way to create spy planes the size of a fist. To do so, they need a model different from that of fixed-wing technology, which governs how airplanes fly. They want to learn how very small things fly. And insects, because they are so tiny, relate to the air differently from birds or planes.

the lingo

aerodynamics—movement through the air

you'll need

Designs of paper airplanes, toy helicopters, and other hovering, flying things, and the materials their construction requires—See *Workshop Resources*, p. 72, for a list of places to get ideas.

Consider materials such as—paper, tulle fabric, plastic bags, gold leaf, mica chips, leaves, film, aluminum foil, mesh, wax, twist ties, paper clips, dead bugs' wings, hard plastic, Mylar, grass, tape, plastic wrap, fish scales, clay, straw, beads, cellophane, sand, balsa wood, glue, playing cards, tissue paper, plastic straws, feathers, seaweed, toothpicks, wire, bone, leather, acrylic, CDs, potato chips, thread, tree bark, paper, a motor, eggshells

Consider small tools such as—tweezers, pins, needles, pencils, nails, bobby pins, matchsticks, paperclips, knives, pins, eyedroppers

what to do

1 **BEGIN WITH A BASIC AIRPLANE OR HELICOPTER SHAPE.** Create one from scratch, basing your model on a box model or designing your own based on a full-size plane or helicopter. Or get a design from one of the resources listed at the end of this workshop.

2 **MAKE THE MODEL WITH SEVERAL DIFFERENT MATERIALS.** Compare them and decide which one would be best adapted to a smaller size.

the QUESTION >> How small a flying machine can you make?

the PLAN >> Build paper airplanes or helicopters, using smaller and smaller measurements, to see how small you can go before the flier stops being able to fly.

3 **MAKE YOUR MODEL ON A SMALLER SCALE.** You may make smaller ones in little increments, or just go straight to cutting, folding, and assembling the smallest parts that you can do.

4 **KEEP A VIDEO RECORD OF YOUR FLIGHTS.**

5 **KEEP CAREFUL NOTES AND RECORDS OF EVERY TOSS.**

6 **KEEP A JOURNAL.** Write about your test flights, errors, changes and adaptations to your design, and outcomes of new attempts.

WORKSHOP RESOURCES >>

Flapping Paper Airplanes: http://www.wikihow.com/Make-a-Flapping-Paper-Airplane

An Interesting Design: http://www.personaltao.com/tao/paperairplane.htm

A Dragonfly: http://www.infosnow.ne.jp/~suzuki-a/meishi/meishie.html

The Online Paper Airplane Museum: http://www.theonlinepaperairplanemuseum.com

The Basic Paper Helicopter: http://users.bigpond.net.au/mechtoys/helicopter.html

Helicopter Variations: http://www.uga.edu/srel/kidsdoscience/sci-method-copters/copter-designs.pdf

Maple Seed Helicopter: http://www.grc.nasa.gov/WWW/K-12/TRC/Aeronautics/Maple_Seed.html

Don't stop here. You've learned so much from your first model that you can bring to future designs. See if you can top your personal best: Make a new design that is smaller, faster, flies farther, and stays in the air longer.

CONSIDER THIS! PRESENT THIS!

Fly your plane or helicopter on site at the science fair, or present a video of the flight.

GO THE EXTRA MILE! Stage a competition among several of your designs.

A CRICKET'S SENSE OF SMELL

(Train an insect to recognize smells)

the basics

BEES, CRICKETS, AND OTHER INSECTS can learn to associate a smell with a reward. This changes the activities of neurons, which are the message pathways through the brain. This can happen quickly, and it can last 24 hours or more after just one reward session.

TIME NEEDED ›
one day

SCIENCE ›
psychology, physiology

SCIENCE CONCEPTS ›
behavior modification, senses

the buzz

The Stealthy Insect Sensor Project is the work of Tim Haarmann of the U.S. Energy Department's Los Alamos National Laboratory in New Mexico. Tim trains bees to sniff out explosives. When the bees are exposed to the odor of explosives, they are given a reward of sugar water. (A bee drinks through its proboscis, uncoiling it like a hose to suck up the sugar water.) After an hour or two of training, the bees respond to the smell of explosives by sticking out their proboscises. A video camera and image recognition software observe whether the bees stick out their proboscises and informs Haarmann when they do.

the lingo

positive reinforcement—a method of changing behavior through rewards

you'll need

crickets (from a pet store), a cricket house, and food—See *Keeping Bugs*, p. 8.
bottle caps
cotton balls
cotton swabs (such as Q-tips)
lids—from two small boxes, such as jewelry boxes
vanilla extract
peppermint extract
water
table salt

the QUESTION >> Can you teach a cricket to recognize a particular smell?

the PLAN >> Try to train live crickets to choose one smell over another.

what to do

 MIX A CUP OF WATER WITH A TEASPOON OF SALT TO MAKE SALINE WATER. You'll need saline water and regular water for this workshop.

2 SET UP TWO SMALL BOX LIDS. In one, place a Q-tip that has been dipped in vanilla and, beside it in a bottle cap, a cotton ball soaked with regular water. In the other box lid, place a Q-tip that has been dipped in peppermint extract and, beside it in a bottle cap, a cotton ball soaked with saline water.

3 PLACE ONE BOX LID IN THE CRICKET HOUSE FOR TEN MINUTES. Every ten minutes, switch the box tops, in this pattern:
10:00: vanilla/regular water
10:10: peppermint/saline water
10:20: vanilla/regular water
10:30: peppermint/saline water

4 OBSERVE HOW MANY CRICKETS INVESTIGATE EACH BOX LID, AND HOW THEY RESPOND.

5 AFTER AN HOUR, TAKE THE WATER OUT OF THE BOX LIDS. Just leave the cotton swabs soaked in vanilla and peppermint extract in the box lids. Put the lids at opposite ends of the aquarium.

Observe the behavior of the crickets. Remove the box lids after ten minutes. Do you think the crickets have learned to identify the vanilla and peppermint? If not, repeat the training, alternating smells for ten minutes at a time for another hour, and then test the crickets again.

> Crickets won't stick out their proboscises (they don't have them). But they should crowd around the water that they prefer once they learn which smell goes with it.

CONSIDER THIS! PRESENT THIS!

> Take photographs or videos of your procedure and the crickets' response, especially the tests.

> **GO THE EXTRA MILE!** Try this experiment with another insect or a pet. How do they compare?

PRESENT IT!

HANDING IT IN, SHOWING IT OFF, telling your story, getting that A. It all comes down to strong science and strong communication. Your presentation tells the story of your work. Tell it well with clear language, visuals, and a little drama.

INCLUDE IT! Include your starting question(s), hypothesis (what you think will happen), purpose (why you're doing this), procedures, tools, data (facts), findings (results), notes, conclusion (decision based on the facts and results), and a follow-up question. Provide a listing of your research: articles, books, websites, interviews, and other information sources you used.

SHOW IT! Drawings, diagrams, graphs, photographs, videos, and PowerPoint presentations tell much more than you can in conversation or writing.

DRAW IT! You're working with visible objects. Learn all you can about them by looking, and then communicate it through artwork. You don't have to be Picasso. Take your time and include all the parts of the bug you are investigating.

GRAPH IT! Computer graphics programs make it easy to put your data into graph form for easy viewing and quick communication of your findings. Check out these websites for making graphs:
- Statistics Canada: http://www.statcan.ca/english/edu/power/ch9/pictograph/picto.htm
- National Center for Education Statistics: www.nces.ed.gov/nceskids/graphing/classic/

POWERPOINT IT! Use a computer to coordinate your graphs, photographs, videos, and other materials into a presentation that's quick to view and easy to understand. You can set up your PowerPoint to loop continually, present it to your teacher on a DVD, and add it to your school portfolio. **Note:** *The Macintosh program Keynote is similar to PowerPoint.*

DRAMATIZE IT! Consider the impact of recordings, dramatic performances, costumes, posters, and sound effects. There's plenty of room for creativity and drama in science.

PHOTOGRAPH IT! Here are some tried-and-true tips for photographing insects:
- JPEGs, TIFFs, or GIFs can all be used to make a slide show. Take four to six digital shots. Then use your computer program (Adobe Photoshop, for example) to create a GIF file out of them. A website like Freedownloadcenter.com shows you how to create a slide show for your laptop or to burn on a CD.
- time lapse, when you want to capture something that takes

Video It
Through a Microscope!

Dr. Shawn Carlson, director of Lab Rats and the Society for the Amateur Scientist, shared this method for turning a regular video camera into a video microscope.

1 Take out the eye lens of the microscope. There are two lenses on the eyepiece tube of the scope. The one at the top is the eye lens, and the one at the bottom is the ocular lens. Unscrew the eye lens and set it aside.

2 Now turn the eyepiece tube over so that the ocular lens is on top. Take a strip of masking tape and wrap it around the eyepiece tube. Important: Usually the eye lens holds the eyepiece up. Without it, the eyepiece could slide into the tube. The tape will keep it snug. Now push the eyepiece back into the scope. The ocular lens is now on top.

3 Use a tripod to position your video camera over the microscope, aiming it to get a clear image.

place over time. Set up a still camera or video camera to take an image every 30 seconds. The result will be a series of still shots that seem to move and change over time.

- video
- A flexi-cam is a camera with a magnifying lens, attached to a TV or computer. Viewers can see a tiny bug, a microscopic organism, a water critter, or other things that are alive and in motion, as well as things that aren't. Track down a flexi-cam in your school's science lab or media room, or see if a local university or educational cooperative has one you can borrow.

the resources

Bugbios: www.bugbios.com

The Bug Guide: http://bugguide.net/node/view/15740

Entomology for Beginners: www.bijlmakers.com/entomology/begin.htm

Insect World, www.insectworld.com, does business in dried insects for collections and for decorations.

Insecta-Inspecta World: www.insecta-inspecta.com

International Society for Arachnology: www.arachnology.org

Iowa State Entomology Index of Internet Resources: http://www.ent.iastate.edu/List/

Smithsonian Institution, National Museum of Natural History, Department of Entomology website: http://entomology.si.edu/

The Virtual Online Butterfly at Live Monarch: http://www.livemonarch.com/adopt.htm

BUG VIDEOS

Microcosmos The directors used tiny cameras they made themselves to get a bug's-eye view. They even made a camera with a miniature helicopter to follow a bee through a forest of wildflowers.

Microcosmos website for free video of all kinds of bugs: http://www.microcosmos.tv/

INSECT SOUNDS

- Environmental Literacy Council: http://www.enviroliteracy.org/subcategory.php/256.html
- Nature Songs: http://www.naturesongs.com/insects.html

MICROSCOPE VIEWS OF BUGS

- Dennis Kunkel has taken many photographs of bugs through a microscope: http://www.denniskunkel.com
- Microangela is a fun site where you can see magnified and colorized photographs of insects, including electron microscope images: http://www.pbrc.hawaii.edu/microangela/
- Bugscope, a University of Illinois, Urbana-Champaign, program, allows students to use scanning electron microscopes (approximate cost: $500,000) from remote locations: http://bugscope.beckman.uiuc.edu/

SCIENCE SUPPLIES

Basic Science Supplies: http://www.basicsciencesupplies.com
Science Stuff: www.sciencestuff.com
Lab Warehouse: www.sciplus.com
Steve Spangler Science: www.stevespanglerscience.com

index